To: ______________________________

From: ______________________________

The LORD is faithful to all his promises
and loving toward all he has made.

Psalm 145:13

Promises for Dads from the New International Version

ISBN 0-310-80065-X

Requests for information should be addressed to:
Inspirio, The gift group of Zondervan
Grand Rapids, Michigan 49530
http://www.inspiriogifts.com

Associate Editor: Molly C. Detweiler
Compiler: Robin S. Schmitt
Designed by: David Carlson & Amy E. Langeler

Printed in China

02 03 04 /HK/ 4 3 2

JANUARY 1

Stand at the crossroads and look;
    ask for the ancient paths,
ask where the good way is, and walk in it,
    and you will find rest for your souls.

Jeremiah 6:16

DECEMBER 31

Now to God who is able to do immeasurably more than all we ask or imagine, according to his power that is at work within us to him be glory in the church and in Christ Jesus throughout all generations, for ever and ever! Amen.

Ephesians 3:20–21

JANUARY 2

Surely God is my help;
the Lord is the one who sustains me.

Psalm 54:4

DECEMBER 30

God has poured out his love into our hearts
by the Holy Spirit, whom he has given us.

Romans 5:5

JANUARY 3

God has given us his very great
and precious promises, so that through them
you may participate in the divine nature.

2 Peter 1:4

DECEMBER 29

"I will pour water on the thirsty land,
and streams on the dry ground;
I will pour out my Spirit on your offspring,
and my blessing on your descendants,"
says the Lord.

Isaiah 44:3

JANUARY 4

Since we are receiving a kingdom that cannot be shaken,
let us be thankful, and so worship God
acceptably with reverence and awe.

Hebrews 12:28

DECEMBER 28

Every good and perfect gift is from above,
coming down from the Father of the heavenly lights,
who does not change like shifting shadows.

James 1:17

JANUARY 5

The Spirit himself testifies with our spirit that we are God's children.

Romans 8:16

DECEMBER 27

Light is shed upon the righteous
and joy on the upright in heart.

Psalm 97:11

JANUARY 6

Praise be to the God and Father of our Lord Jesus Christ, the Father of compassion and the God of all comfort, who comforts us in all our troubles, so that we can comfort those in any trouble with the comfort we ourselves have received from God. For just as the sufferings of Christ flow over into our lives, so also through Christ our comfort overflows.

2 Corinthians 1:3–5

DECEMBER 26

The Word became flesh and made his dwelling among us.
We have seen his glory, the glory of the One and Only,
who came from the Father, full of grace and truth.

John 1:14

JANUARY 7

You guide me with your counsel, O Lord,
and afterward you will take me into glory.

Psalm 73:24

DECEMBER 25

To us a child is born,
    to us a son is given,
    and the government will be on his shoulders.
And he will be called
    Wonderful Counselor, Mighty God,
    Everlasting Father, Prince of Peace.

Isaiah 9:6

JANUARY 8

Jesus said, "When he, the Spirit of truth, comes, he will guide you into all truth. He will not speak on his own; he will speak only what he hears, and he will tell you what is yet to come."

John 16:13

DECEMBER 24

The virgin will be with child and will give birth to a son, and they will call him Immanuel—which means, "God with us."

Matthew 1:23

JANUARY 9

In Christ we who are many form one body,
and each member belongs to all the others.
We have different gifts, according to the grace given us.

Romans 12:5–6

DECEMBER 23

The fear of the LORD is the beginning of wisdom;
all who follow his precepts have good understanding.
To him belongs eternal praise.

Psalm 111:10

JANUARY 10

May the LORD, the God of your fathers, increase you a thousand times and bless you as he has promised!

Deuteronomy 1:11

DECEMBER 22

May the LORD make you increase,
both you and your children.

Psalm 115:14

JANUARY 11

"They will call on my name
and I will answer them;
I will say, 'They are my people,'
and they will say, 'The LORD is our God,'"
says the Lord.

Zechariah 13:9

DECEMBER 21

If we walk in the light, as Christ is in the light,
we have fellowship with one another, and the blood of Jesus,
his Son, purifies us from all sin.

1 John 1:7

JANUARY 12

When the kindness and love of God our Savior appeared,
he saved us, not because of righteous things we had done,
but because of his mercy.

Titus 3:4–5

DECEMBER 20

You will call, and the LORD will answer;
you will cry for help, and he will say: Here am I.

Isaiah 58:9

JANUARY 13

The blessing of the LORD brings wealth,
and he adds no trouble to it.

Proverbs 10:22

DECEMBER 19

My frame was not hidden from you, Lord,
when I was made in the secret place.
When I was woven together in the depths of the earth,
your eyes saw my unformed body.
All the days ordained for me were written in your book
before one of them came to be.

Psalm 139:15–16

JANUARY 14

The LORD watches over
the way of the righteous.

Psalm 1:6

DECEMBER 18

Train a child in the way he should go,
and when he is old he will not turn from it.

Proverbs 22:6

JANUARY 15

"Though the mountains be shaken
 and the hills be removed,
yet my unfailing love for you will not be shaken
 nor my covenant of peace be removed,"
 says the LORD, who has compassion on you.

Isaiah 54:10

DECEMBER 17

I commit you to God and to the word of his grace, which can build you up and give you an inheritance among all those who are sanctified.

Acts 20:32

JANUARY 16

Do not fear, for I am with you;
do not be dismayed, for I am your God.
I will strengthen you and help you;
I will uphold you with my righteous right hand.

Isaiah 41:10

DECEMBER 16

Though you have not seen Christ, you love him;
and even though you do not see him now, you believe in him
and are filled with an inexpressible and glorious joy,
for you are receiving the goal of your faith,
the salvation of your souls.

1 Peter 1:8–9

JANUARY 17

Jesus said, "Everyone who hears these words of mine and puts them into practice is like a wise man who built his house on the rock. The rain came down, the streams rose, and the winds blew and beat against that house; yet it did not fall, because it had its foundation on the rock."

Matthew 7:24–25

DECEMBER 15

Stand firm. Let nothing move you.
Always give yourselves fully to the work of the Lord,
because you know that your labor in the Lord is not in vain.

1 Corinthians 15:58

JANUARY 18

Preserve sound judgment and discernment,
do not let them out of your sight;
they will be life for you,
an ornament to grace your neck.

Proverbs 3:21–22

DECEMBER 14

Many, O LORD my God,
are the wonders you have done.
The things you planned for us
no one can recount to you;
were I to speak and tell of them,
they would be too many to declare.

Psalm 40:5

JANUARY 19

God is able to make all grace abound to you,
so that in all things at all times, having all that you need,
you will abound in every good work.

2 Corinthians 9:8

DECEMBER 13

May your unfailing love be my comfort, O Lord,
according to your promise.

Psalm 119:76

JANUARY 20

Commit your way to the LORD;
trust in him and he will do this:
He will make your righteousness shine like the dawn,
the justice of your cause like the noonday sun.

Psalm 37:5–6

DECEMBER 12

Our sons in their youth
will be like well-nurtured plants,
and our daughters will be like pillars
carved to adorn a palace. . . .
Blessed are the people of whom this is true;
blessed are the people whose God is the LORD.

Psalm 144:12, 15

JANUARY 21

The mind of sinful man is death,
but the mind controlled by the Spirit is life and peace.

Romans 8:6

DECEMBER 11

In your unfailing love you will lead
 the people you have redeemed, O Lord.
In your strength you will guide them
 to your holy dwelling.

Exodus 15:13

JANUARY 22

Let everyone who is godly pray to you, Lord,
while you may be found;
surely when the mighty waters rise,
they will not reach him.

Psalm 32:6

DECEMBER 10

Because of the LORD's great love we are not consumed,
for his compassions never fail.

Lamentations 3:22

JANUARY 23

Blessed is the man who fears the LORD,
who finds great delight in his commands.
His children will be mighty in the land;
the generation of the upright will be blessed.

Psalm 112:1–2

DECEMBER 9

Let the morning bring me word
of your unfailing love, O Lord,
for I have put my trust in you.
Show me the way I should go,
for to you I lift up my soul.

Psalm 143:8

JANUARY 24

Two are better than one,
    because they have a good return for their work:
If one falls down,
    his friend can help him up.

Ecclesiastes 4:9–10

DECEMBER 8

We, who with unveiled faces all reflect the Lord's glory,
are being transformed into his likeness
with ever-increasing glory, which comes from the Lord,
who is the Spirit.

2 Corinthians 3:18

JANUARY 25

The Lord will cover you with his feathers,
and under his wings you will find refuge;
his faithfulness will be your shield and rampart.

Psalm 91:4

DECEMBER 7

You are my lamp, O LORD;
the LORD turns my darkness into light.
With your help I can advance against a troop;
with my God I can scale a wall.

2 Samuel 22:29–30

JANUARY 26

We tell you the good news: What God promised our fathers he has fulfilled for us, their children, by raising up Jesus. As it is written in the second Psalm:

"You are my Son;
today I have become your Father."

Acts 13:32–33

DECEMBER 6

May our Lord Jesus Christ himself and God our Father,
who loved us and by his grace gave us eternal encouragement
and good hope, encourage your hearts and
strengthen you in every good deed and word.

2 Thessalonians 2:16–17

JANUARY 27

Because you are my help,
I sing in the shadow of your wings, O Lord.
My soul clings to you;
your right hand upholds me.

Psalm 63:7–8

DECEMBER 5

Delight yourself in the LORD
and he will give you the desires of your heart.

Psalm 37:4

JANUARY 28

God made Christ who had no sin to be sin for us,
so that in him we might become the righteousness of God.

2 Corinthians 5:21

DECEMBER 4

"I will bless [my people] and the places surrounding my hill.
I will send down showers in season;
there will be showers of blessing," says the Lord.

Ezekiel 34:26

JANUARY 29

Teach me to do your will,
for you are my God;
may your good Spirit
lead me on level ground.

Psalm 143:10

DECEMBER 3

Christ is the mediator of a new covenant,
that those who are called may receive the promised eternal inheritance—now that he has died as a ransom to set them free from the sins committed under the first covenant.

Hebrews 9:15

JANUARY 30

May all who seek you
rejoice and be glad in you;
may those who love your salvation always say,
"The LORD be exalted!"

Psalm 40:16

DECEMBER 2

The world or life or death
or the present or the future—all are yours,
and you are of Christ, and Christ is of God.

1 Corinthians 3:22–23

JANUARY 31

If the many died by the trespass of the one man,
how much more did God's grace and the gift
that came by the grace of the one man, Jesus Christ,
overflow to the many!

Romans 5:15

DECEMBER 1

Whatever you do, work at it with all your heart,
as working for the Lord, not for men,
since you know that you will receive an inheritance
from the Lord as a reward.
It is the Lord Christ you are serving.

Colossians 3:23–24

FEBRUARY 1

Let us not become weary in doing good,
for at the proper time we will reap a harvest
if we do not give up.

Galatians 6:9

NOVEMBER 30

May those who fear you, Lord,
rejoice when they see me,
for I have put my hope in your word. . . .
You are my refuge and my shield;
I have put my hope in your word.

Psalm 119:74, 114

FEBRUARY 2

No one whose hope is in you, Lord,
will ever be put to shame.

Psalm 25:3

NOVEMBER 29

I have set the LORD always before me.
Because he is at my right hand,
I will not be shaken.

Psalm 16:8

FEBRUARY 3

God put a new song in my mouth,
a hymn of praise to our God.
Many will see and fear
and put their trust in the LORD.

Psalm 40:3

NOVEMBER 28

Do not forsake wisdom, and she will protect you;
love her, and she will watch over you.

Proverbs 4:6

FEBRUARY 4

Discipline your son, for in that there is hope. . . .
Discipline your son, and he will give you peace;
he will bring delight to your soul.

Proverbs 19:18; 29:17

NOVEMBER 27

Do not throw away your confidence;
it will be richly rewarded.
You need to persevere so that when you have done
the will of God, you will receive what he has promised.

Hebrews 10:35–36

FEBRUARY 5

Wisdom is supreme; therefore get wisdom.
    Though it cost all you have, get understanding.
Esteem her, and she will exalt you;
    embrace her, and she will honor you.
She will set a garland of grace on your head
    and present you with a crown of splendor.

Proverbs 4:7–9

NOVEMBER 26

We always thank God for . . . you, mentioning you in our prayers.
We continually remember before our God and Father
your work produced by faith, your labor prompted by love,
and your endurance inspired by hope in our Lord Jesus Christ.

1 Thessalonians 1:2–3

FEBRUARY 6

Come, let us bow down in worship,
  let us kneel before the LORD our Maker.
for he is our God and we are the people of his pasture,
  the flock under his care.

Psalm 95:6–7

NOVEMBER 25

Enter his gates with thanksgiving
and his courts with praise;
give thanks to him and praise his name.
For the LORD is good and his love endures forever;
his faithfulness continues through all generations.

Psalm 100:4–5

FEBRUARY 7

There remains, then, a Sabbath-rest for the people of God; for anyone who enters God's rest also rests from his own work, just as God did from his. Let us, therefore, make every effort to enter that rest.

Hebrews 4:9–11

NOVEMBER 24

God so loved the world that he gave his one and only Son, that whoever believes in him shall not perish but have eternal life.

John 3:16

FEBRUARY 8

The truly righteous man attains life.

Proverbs 11:19

NOVEMBER 23

You know with all your heart and soul that not one of all the good promises the LORD your God gave you has failed. Every promise has been fulfilled; not one has failed.

Joshua 23:14

FEBRUARY 9

You are forgiving and good, O Lord,
abounding in love to all who call to you.

Psalm 86:5

NOVEMBER 22

Your sun will never set again,
and your moon will wane no more;
the LORD will be your everlasting light,
and your days of sorrow will end.

Isaiah 60:20

FEBRUARY 10

Do any of the worthless idols of the nations bring rain?
Do the skies themselves send down showers?
No, it is you, O LORD our God.
Therefore our hope is in you,
for you are the one who does all this.

Jeremiah 14:22

NOVEMBER 21

I cry out to God Most High,
    to God, who fulfills his purpose for me.
He sends from heaven and saves me, . . .
    God sends his love and his faithfulness.

Psalm 57:2–3

FEBRUARY 11

"I will give them singleness of heart and action, so that they will always fear me for their own good and the good of their children after them," says the Lord.

Jeremiah 32:39

NOVEMBER 20

The one who plants and the one who waters
have one purpose, and each will be rewarded according
to their own labor. For we are God's fellow workers;
you are God's field, God's building.

1 Corinthians 3:8–9

FEBRUARY 12

A righteous man may have many troubles,
but the LORD delivers him from them all.

Psalm 34:19

NOVEMBER 19

The LORD will guide you always;
he will satisfy your needs in a sun-scorched land
and will strengthen your frame.
You will be like a well-watered garden,
like a spring whose waters never fail.

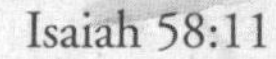

Isaiah 58:11

FEBRUARY 13

This is what God promised us—even eternal life.

1 John 2:25

NOVEMBER 18

"I will heal my people and
will let them enjoy abundant peace
and security," says the Lord.

Jeremiah 33:6

FEBRUARY 14

Love is patient, love is kind. It does not envy, it does not boast, it is not proud. It is not rude, it is not self-seeking, it is not easily angered, it keeps no record of wrongs. Love does not delight in evil but rejoices with the truth. It always protects, always trusts, always hopes, always perseveres. Love never fails.

1 Corinthians 13:4–8

NOVEMBER 17

I pray that you, being rooted and established in love, may have power, together with all the saints, to grasp how wide and long and high and deep is the love of Christ, and to know this love that surpasses knowledge—that you may be filled to the measure of all the fullness of God.

Ephesians 3:17–19

FEBRUARY 15

Because of his great love for us, God,
who is rich in mercy, made us alive with Christ
even when we were dead in transgressions—
it is by grace you have been saved.

Ephesians 2:4–5

NOVEMBER 16

Rejoice and be glad, because great
is your reward in heaven.

Matthew 5:12

FEBRUARY 16

This is what the LORD says—
your Redeemer, the Holy One of Israel:
"I am the LORD your God,
who teaches you what is best for you,
who directs you in the way you should go."

Isaiah 48:17

NOVEMBER 15

"Before [my people] call I will answer;
while they are still speaking I will hear,"
says the Lord.

Isaiah 65:24

FEBRUARY 17

The LORD is with you when you are with him.
If you seek him, he will be found by you.

2 Chronicles 15:2

NOVEMBER 14

"Because he loves me," says the LORD, "I will rescue him;
I will protect him, for he acknowledges my name."

Psalm 91:14

FEBRUARY 18

God who began a good work
in you will carry it on to completion
until the day of Christ Jesus.

Philippians 1:6

NOVEMBER 13

The body is a unit, though it is made up of many parts; and though all its parts are many, they form one body. So it is with Christ. For we were all baptized by one Spirit into one body—whether Jews or Greeks, slave or free—and we were all given the one Spirit to drink.

1 Corinthians 12:12–13

You are a shield around me, O Lord;
you bestow glory on me and lift up my head.

Psalm 3:3

NOVEMBER 12

"I know the plans I have for you," declares the LORD,
"plans to prosper you and not to harm you,
plans to give you hope and a future."

Jeremiah 29:11

FEBRUARY 20

In keeping with God's promise
we are looking forward to a new heaven and
a new earth, the home of righteousness.

2 Peter 3:13

NOVEMBER 11

A cheerful look brings joy to the heart.

Proverbs 15:30

FEBRUARY 21

Repent and be baptized, every one of you,
in the name of Jesus Christ for the forgiveness of your sins.
And you will receive the gift of the Holy Spirit.
The promise is for you and your children
and for all who are far off—for
all whom the Lord our God will call.

Acts 2:38–39

NOVEMBER 10

Whatever you ask for in prayer,
believe that you have received it,
and it will be yours.

Mark 11:24

FEBRUARY 22

I will lie down and sleep in peace,
for you alone, O LORD,
make me dwell in safety.

Psalm 4:8

NOVEMBER 9

Taste and see that the LORD is good;
blessed is the man who takes refuge in him.

Psalm 34:8

FEBRUARY 23

Jesus said, "Here I am! I stand at the door and knock.
If anyone hears my voice and opens the door,
I will come in and eat with him, and he with me."

Revelation 3:20

NOVEMBER 8

Be patient . . . until the Lord's coming.
See how the farmer waits for the land to yield
its valuable crop and how patient he is for the autumn
and spring rains. You too, be patient and stand firm,
because the Lord's coming is near.

James 5:7–8

FEBRUARY 24

"I will give them a heart to know me,
that I am the LORD. They will be my people,
and I will be their God," says the LORD.

Jeremiah 24:7

NOVEMBER 7

God is our God for ever and ever;
he will be our guide even to the end.

Psalm 48:14

FEBRUARY 25

Pleasant words are a honeycomb,
sweet to the soul and healing to the bones.

Proverbs 16:24

NOVEMBER 6

Those who walk uprightly
enter into peace.

Isaiah 57:2

FEBRUARY 26

In repentance and rest is your salvation,
in quietness and trust is your strength.

Isaiah 30:15

NOVEMBER 5

May you be richly rewarded by the LORD, the God of Israel, under whose wings you have come to take refuge.

Ruth 2:12

FEBRUARY 27

The Lord is faithful, and he will strengthen and protect you from the evil one.

2 Thessalonians 3:3

NOVEMBER 4

"You will call upon me and come and pray
to me, and I will listen to you.
You will seek me and find me when
you seek me with all your heart," says the Lord.

Jeremiah 29:12–13

FEBRUARY 28

Jesus said, "I tell you the truth,
my Father will give you whatever you ask in my name.
Until now you have not asked for anything in my name.
Ask and you will receive, and your joy will be complete."

John 16:23–24

NOVEMBER 3

I call to God,
and the LORD saves me.
Evening, morning and noon
I cry out in distress,
and he hears my voice.

Psalm 55:16–17

FEBRUARY 29

Christ himself is our peace, who has made the two one and has destroyed the barrier, the dividing wall of hostility, by abolishing in his flesh the law with its commandments and regulations. His purpose was to create in himself one new man out of the two, thus making peace.

Ephesians 2:14–15

NOVEMBER 2

Jesus said, "Whoever does the will of my Father in heaven is my brother and sister and mother."

Matthew 12:50

MARCH 1

May the Lord make your love increase
and overflow for each other.

1 Thessalonians 3:12

NOVEMBER 1

LORD, you have assigned me my portion and my cup;
you have made my lot secure.
The boundary lines have fallen for me in pleasant places;
surely I have a delightful inheritance.

Psalm 16:5–6

MARCH 2

Let all who take refuge in you be glad, LORD;
  let them ever sing for joy.
Spread your protection over them,
  that those who love your name may rejoice in you.

Psalm 5:11

OCTOBER 31

Is any one of you in trouble? He should pray. Is anyone happy? Let him sing songs of praise. Is any one of you sick? He should call the elders of the church to pray over him and anoint him with oil in the name of the Lord. And the prayer offered in faith will make the sick person well; the Lord will raise him up.

James 5:13–15

MARCH 3

The LORD is near to all who call on him,
to all who call on him in truth.

Psalm 145:18

OCTOBER 30

"I will be a Father to you,
and you will be my sons and daughters,"
says the Lord Almighty.

2 Corinthians 6:18

MARCH 4

Jesus said, “I am the vine; you are the branches.
If a man remains in me and I in him, he will bear much fruit.”

John 15:5

OCTOBER 29

The Lord stilled the storm to a whisper;
the waves of the sea were hushed.
They were glad when it grew calm,
and he guided them to their desired haven.
Let them give thanks to the LORD for his unfailing love
and his wonderful deeds for men.

Psalm 107:29–31

MARCH 5

You are my hiding place, Lord;
you will protect me from trouble
and surround me with songs of deliverance.

Psalm 32:7

OCTOBER 28

One thing I ask of the LORD,
    this is what I seek:
that I may dwell in the house of the LORD
    all the days of my life,
to gaze upon the beauty of the LORD
    and to seek him in his temple.

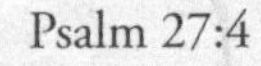

Psalm 27:4

MARCH 6

God redeemed us in order that the blessing given to Abraham might come to the Gentiles through Christ Jesus, so that by faith we might receive the promise of the Spirit.

Galatians 3:14

OCTOBER 27

No discipline seems pleasant at the time, but painful. Later on, however, it produces a harvest of righteousness and peace for those who have been trained by it.

Hebrews 12:11

MARCH 7

God created man in his own image,
in the image of God he created him;
male and female he created them.

God blessed them and said to them, "Be fruitful and increase in number."

Genesis 1:27–28

OCTOBER 26

The precepts of the LORD are right,
giving joy to the heart.
The commands of the LORD are radiant,
giving light to the eyes.

Psalm 19:8

MARCH 8

You are all sons of God through faith in Christ Jesus, for all of you who were baptized into Christ have clothed yourselves with Christ. There is neither Jew nor Greek, slave nor free, male nor female, for you are all one in Christ Jesus. If you belong to Christ, then you are Abraham's seed, and heirs according to the promise.

Galatians 3:26–29

OCTOBER 25

Jesus himself bore our sins in his body on the tree,
so that we might die to sins and live for righteousness;
by his wounds you have been healed.

1 Peter 2:24

MARCH 9

Dear friends, now we are children of God,
and what we will be has not yet been made known.
But we know that when he appears, we shall be like him,
for we shall see him as he is. Everyone who has
this hope in him purifies himself, just as he is pure.

1 John 3:2–3

OCTOBER 24

The Messiah was pierced for our transgressions,
he was crushed for our iniquities;
the punishment that brought us peace was upon him,
and by his wounds we are healed.

Isaiah 53:5

MARCH 10

"I will lead the blind by ways they have not known,
along unfamiliar paths I will guide them;
I will turn the darkness into light before them
and make the rough places smooth.
These are the things I will do;
I will not forsake them," says the Lord.

Isaiah 42:16

OCTOBER 23

Wisdom is sweet to your soul;
 if you find it, there is a future hope for you,
 and your hope will not be cut off.

Proverbs 24:14

MARCH 11

Praise the LORD, O my soul,
and forget not all his benefits . . .
who satisfies your desires with good things
so that your youth is renewed like the eagle's.

Psalm 103:2, 5

OCTOBER 22

Praise be to the God and Father of our Lord Jesus Christ!
In his great mercy he has given us new birth into a living hope
through the resurrection of Jesus Christ from the dead,
and into an inheritance that can never perish, spoil or fade—
kept in heaven for you.

1 Peter 1:3–4

MARCH 12

God will command his angels concerning you
  to guard you in all your ways;
they will lift you up in their hands,
  so that you will not strike your foot against a stone.

Psalm 91:11–12

OCTOBER 21

Gold there is, and rubies in abundance,
but lips that speak knowledge are a rare jewel.

Proverbs 20:15

MARCH 13

When I called, you answered me. Lord;
you made me bold and stouthearted.

Psalm 138:3

OCTOBER 20

The Lord heals the brokenhearted
and binds up their wounds.

Psalm 147:3

MARCH 14

I was young and now I am old,
 yet I have never seen the righteous forsaken
 or their children begging bread.
They are always generous and lend freely;
 their children will be blessed.

Psalm 37:25–26

OCTOBER 19

It is God who arms me with strength
  and makes my way perfect.
He makes my feet like the feet of a deer;
  he enables me to stand on the heights.

Psalm 18:32–33

MARCH 15

Jesus said, "I am the resurrection and the life. He who believes in me will live, even though he dies."

John 11:25

OCTOBER 18

"I will gather you; . . .
I will bring you home.
I will give you honor and praise
among all the peoples of the earth
when I restore your fortunes
before your very eyes,"
says the LORD.

Zephaniah 3:20

MARCH 16

The LORD God is a sun and shield;
the LORD bestows favor and honor;
no good thing does he withhold
from those whose walk is blameless.

Psalm 84:11

OCTOBER 17

Jesus said, "As the Father has loved me, so have I loved you. Now remain in my love. If you obey my commands, you will remain in my love, just as I have obeyed my Father's commands and remain in his love. I have told you this so that my joy may be in you and that your joy may be complete."

John 15:9-11

MARCH 17

You shall rejoice in all the good things
the LORD your God has given to you and your household.

Deuteronomy 26:11

OCTOBER 16

"My Presence will go with you,
and I will give you rest," says the LORD.

Exodus 33:14

MARCH 18

Store up for yourselves treasures in heaven, where moth and rust do not destroy, and where thieves do not break in and steal. For where your treasure is, there your heart will be also.

Matthew 6:20–21

OCTOBER 15

You still the hunger of those you cherish, LORD;
their sons have plenty,
and they store up wealth for their children.

Psalm 17:14

MARCH 19

Give, and it will be given to you.
A good measure, pressed down,
shaken together and running over,
will be poured into your lap.
For with the measure you use,
it will be measured to you.

Luke 6:38

OCTOBER 14

Let the beloved of the LORD rest secure in him,
for he shields him all day long,
and the one the LORD loves rests between his shoulders.

Deuteronomy 33:12

MARCH 20

Blessed is the man who perseveres under trial,
because when he has stood the test,
he will receive the crown of life
that God has promised to those who love him.

James 1:12

OCTOBER 13

The LORD is a refuge for the oppressed,
a stronghold in times of trouble.
Those who know your name will trust in you,
for you, LORD, have never forsaken those who seek you.

Psalm 9:9–10

MARCH 21

Since you are my rock and my fortress, Lord,
for the sake of your name lead and guide me.

Psalm 31:3

OCTOBER 12

Show me your ways, O LORD,
teach me your paths;
guide me in your truth and teach me,
for you are God my Savior,
and my hope is in you all day long.

Psalm 25:4–5

MARCH 22

All have sinned and fall short of the glory of God,
and are justified freely by his grace
through the redemption that came by Christ Jesus.

Romans 3:23–24

OCTOBER 11

Jesus said, "I no longer call you servants, because a servant does not know his master's business. Instead, I have called you friends, for everything that I learned from my Father I have made known to you."

John 15:15

MARCH 23

Grace, mercy and peace from God the Father
and from Jesus Christ, the Father's Son,
will be with us in truth and love.

2 John 1:3

OCTOBER 10

"I guide you in the way of wisdom
and lead you along straight paths," says the Lord.

Proverbs 4:11

MARCH 24

In Christ you too are being built together
to become a dwelling in which God lives by his Spirit.

Ephesians 2:22

OCTOBER 9

Though we live in the world, we do not wage war as the world does. The weapons we fight with are not the weapons of the world. On the contrary, they have divine power to demolish strongholds.

2 Corinthians 10:3–4

MARCH 25

May God himself, the God of peace, sanctify you through and through. May your whole spirit, soul and body be kept blameless at the coming of our Lord Jesus Christ. The one who calls you is faithful and he will do it.

1 Thessalonians 5:23–24

OCTOBER 8

Blessed are they who keep God's statutes
and seek him with all their heart.

Psalm 119:2

MARCH 26

Through the gospel the Gentiles are heirs together with Israel, members together of one body, and sharers together in the promise in Christ Jesus.

Ephesians 3:6

OCTOBER 7

You care for the land and water it, Lord;
you enrich it abundantly.
The streams of God are filled with water
to provide the people with grain,
for so you have ordained it.

Psalm 65:9

MARCH 27

The joy of the LORD is your strength.

Nehemiah 8:10

OCTOBER 6

Remember this: Whoever sows sparingly
will also reap sparingly, and whoever sows generously
will also reap generously. Each man should give
what he has decided in his heart to give, not reluctantly
or under compulsion, for God loves a cheerful giver.

2 Corinthians 9:6–7

MARCH 28

Even in darkness light dawns for the upright,
for the gracious and compassionate and righteous man.

Psalm 112:4

OCTOBER 5

Jesus said, “In my Father’s house are many rooms;
if it were not so, I would have told you.
I am going there to prepare a place for you.
And if I go and prepare a place for you,
I will come back and take you to be with me
that you also may be where I am.”

John 14:2–3

MARCH 29

Whether you turn to the right or to the left,
your ears will hear a voice behind you,
saying, “This is the way; walk in it.”

Isaiah 30:21

OCTOBER 4

The righteousness of the blameless
makes a straight way for them.

Proverbs 11:5

MARCH 30

I lie down and sleep;
I wake again, because the LORD sustains me.

Psalm 3:5

OCTOBER 3

We wait in hope for the LORD;
he is our help and our shield.

Psalm 33:20

MARCH 31

O LORD my God, I called to you for help
and you healed me.

Psalm 30:2

OCTOBER 2

Praise be to the LORD,
for he showed his wonderful love to me
when I was in a besieged city.
In my alarm I said,
"I am cut off from your sight!"
Yet you heard my cry for mercy
when I called to you for help.

Psalm 31:21–22

APRIL 1

If you, O LORD, kept a record of sins,
O Lord, who could stand?
But with you there is forgiveness;
therefore you are feared.
I wait for the LORD, my soul waits,
and in his word I put my hope.

Psalm 130:3–5

OCTOBER 1

How great is your goodness, O Lord,
which you have stored up for those who fear you,
which you bestow in the sight of men
on those who take refuge in you.

Psalm 31:19

APRIL 2

I will praise you, O Lord, among the nations;
I will sing of you among the peoples.
For great is your love, reaching to the heavens;
your faithfulness reaches to the skies.

Psalm 57:9–10

SEPTEMBER 30

Jesus said, "If two of you on earth
agree about anything you ask for,
it will be done for you by my Father in heaven."

Matthew 18:19

APRIL 3

We have confidence before God
and receive from him anything we ask,
because we obey his commands
and do what pleases him.

1 John 3:21–22

SEPTEMBER 29

The LORD is faithful to all his promises
and loving toward all he has made.

Psalm 145:13

APRIL 4

The LORD will fight for you;
you need only to be still.

Exodus 14:14

SEPTEMBER 28

As you know, we consider blessed those who have persevered. You have heard of Job's perseverance and have seen what the Lord finally brought about. The Lord is full of compassion and mercy.

James 5:11

APRIL 5

Let the heavens rejoice, let the earth be glad;
    let the sea resound, and all that is in it;
let the fields be jubilant, and everything in them.
Then all the trees of the forest will sing for joy;
they will sing before the LORD, for he comes,
    he comes to judge the earth.
He will judge the world in righteousness
    and the peoples in his truth.

Psalm 96:11–13

SEPTEMBER 27

God will keep you strong to the end,
so that you will be blameless on the day
of our Lord Jesus Christ.

1 Corinthians 1:8

APRIL 6

I wait for you, O LORD;
you will answer, O Lord my God.

Psalm 38:15

SEPTEMBER 26

Your righteousness is like the mighty mountains,
your justice like the great deep.
O LORD, you preserve both man and beast.

Psalm 36:6

APRIL 7

The lions may grow weak and hungry,
but those who seek the LORD lack no good thing.

Psalm 34:10

May God strengthen your hearts so that you will be blameless and holy in the presence of our God and Father when our Lord Jesus comes with all his holy ones.

1 Thessalonians 3:13

APRIL 8

From the fullness of God's grace we have all received one blessing after another.

John 1:16

SEPTEMBER 24

The LORD bless you
and keep you;
the LORD make his face shine upon you
and be gracious to you;
the LORD turn his face toward you
and give you peace.

Numbers 6:24–26

APRIL 9

Children's children are a crown to the aged,
and parents are the pride of their children.

Proverbs 17:6

SEPTEMBER 23

Jesus said, "Since you have kept my command
to endure patiently, I will also keep you
from the hour of trial that is going to come upon
the whole world to test those who live on the earth."

Revelation 3:10

APRIL 10

"I will instruct you and teach you in the way you should go," says the Lord.

Psalm 32:8

SEPTEMBER 22

In the presence of the LORD your God,
you and your families shall eat and shall rejoice
in everything you have put your hand to,
because the LORD your God has blessed you.

Deuteronomy 12:7

APRIL 11

As you come to Christ, the living Stone—
rejected by men but chosen by God
and precious to him—you also, like living stones,
are being built into a spiritual house
to be a holy priesthood, offering spiritual sacrifices
acceptable to God through Jesus Christ.

1 Peter 2:4–5

SEPTEMBER 21

The LORD will keep you from all harm —
he will watch over your life;
the LORD will watch over your coming and going
both now and forevermore.

Psalm 121:7–8

APRIL 12

Jesus said, "Take my yoke upon you and learn from me, for I am gentle and humble in heart, and you will find rest for your souls. For my yoke is easy and my burden is light."

Matthew 11:29–30

SEPTEMBER 20

"For you who revere my name, the sun of righteousness will rise with healing in its wings," says the Lord.

Malachi 4:2

APRIL 13

God is our refuge and strength,
an ever-present help in trouble.

Psalm 46:1

SEPTEMBER 19

The Lord will yet fill your mouth with laughter
and your lips with shouts of joy.

Job 8:21

APRIL 14

How gracious God will be when you cry for help!
As soon as he hears, he will answer you.

Isaiah 30:19

SEPTEMBER 18

If any of you lacks wisdom, he should ask God,
who gives generously to all without finding fault,
and it will be given to him.

James 1:5

APRIL 15

When I am afraid,
I will trust in you.
In God, whose word I praise,
in God I trust; I will not be afraid.
What can mortal man do to me?

Psalm 56:3–4

SEPTEMBER 17

Those who hope in the LORD
will renew their strength.
They will soar on wings like eagles;
they will run and not grow weary,
they will walk and not be faint.

Isaiah 40:31

APRIL 16

May the God of hope fill you with all joy
and peace as you trust in him.

Romans 15:13

SEPTEMBER 16

When I said, "My foot is slipping,"
your love, O LORD, supported me.
When anxiety was great within me,
your consolation brought joy to my soul.

Psalm 94:18–19

APRIL 17

Sons are a heritage from the LORD,
children a reward from him.

Psalm 127:3

SEPTEMBER 15

The LORD has heard my cry for mercy;
the LORD accepts my prayer.

Psalm 6:9

APRIL 18

The ransomed of the LORD will return.
They will enter Zion with singing;
  everlasting joy will crown their heads.
Gladness and joy will overtake them,
  and sorrow and sighing will flee away.

Isaiah 35:10

SEPTEMBER 14

I can do everything through Christ
who gives me strength.

Philippians 4:13

APRIL 19

I will fear no evil,
for you are with me, O Lord;
your rod and your staff,
they comfort me.

Psalm 23:4

SEPTEMBER 13

God has shown kindness by giving you
rain from heaven and crops in their seasons;
he provides you with plenty of food
and fills your hearts with joy.

Acts 14:17

APRIL 20

The eternal God is your refuge,
and underneath are the everlasting arms.

Deuteronomy 33:27

SEPTEMBER 12

Like arrows in the hands of a warrior
are sons born in one's youth.
Blessed is the man
whose quiver is full of them.

Psalm 127:4–5

APRIL 21

The LORD will fulfill his purpose for me;
your love, O LORD, endures forever.

Psalm 138:8

SEPTEMBER 11

When you pass through the waters,
I will be with you;
and when you pass through the rivers,
they will not sweep over you.
When you walk through the fire,
you will not be burned;
the flames will not set you ablaze.
For I am the LORD, your God.

Isaiah 43:2–3

APRIL 22

Let us hold unswervingly to the hope we profess,
for God who promised is faithful.

Hebrews 10:23

SEPTEMBER 10

If you make the Most High your dwelling —
even the LORD, who is my refuge —
then no harm will befall you,
no disaster will come near your tent.

Psalm 91:9–10

If we confess our sins, God is faithful
and just and will forgive us our sins
and purify us from all unrighteousness.

1 John 1:9

SEPTEMBER 9

Your kingdom is an everlasting kingdom, O God,
and your dominion endures through all generations.

Psalm 145:13

APRIL 24

Faithfulness springs forth from the earth,
  and righteousness looks down from heaven.
The LORD will indeed give what is good,
  and our land will yield its harvest.

Psalm 85:11–12

SEPTEMBER 8

Trust in the LORD with all your heart
    and lean not on your own understanding;
in all your ways acknowledge him,
    and he will make your paths straight.

Proverbs 3:5–6

APRIL 25

You will be made rich in every way
so that you can be generous
on every occasion, and . . . your generosity
will result in thanksgiving to God.

2 Corinthians 9:11

SEPTEMBER 7

God did not give us a spirit of timidity,
but a spirit of power,
of love and of self-discipline.

2 Timothy 1:7

APRIL 26

"I will give you shepherds after my own heart, who will lead you with knowledge and understanding," says the Lord.

Jeremiah 3:15

SEPTEMBER 6

The LORD your God will
bless you in all your harvest
and in all the work of your hands,
and your joy will be complete.

Deuteronomy 16:15

APRIL 27

You will keep in perfect peace
him whose mind is steadfast,
because he trusts in you, Lord.

Isaiah 26:3

SEPTEMBER 5

How great is the love the Father has lavished on us, that we should be called children of God!

1 John 3:1

APRIL 28

God chose to give us birth
through the word of truth,
that we might be a kind
of firstfruits of all he created.

James 1:18

SEPTEMBER 4

Let love and faithfulness never leave you;
bind them around your neck,
write them on the tablet of your heart.
Then you will win favor and a good name
in the sight of God and man.

Proverbs 3:3–4

APRIL 29

I am convinced that neither death nor life,
neither angels nor demons,
neither the present nor the future,
nor any powers, neither height nor depth,
nor anything else in all creation,
will be able to separate us from the love of God
that is in Christ Jesus our Lord.

Romans 8:38–39

SEPTEMBER 3

Jesus took a little child and had him stand among them.
Taking him in his arms, he said to them,
"Whoever welcomes one of these little children
in my name welcomes me; and whoever welcomes me
does not welcome me but the one who sent me."

Mark 9:36–37

APRIL 30

The Spirit helps us in our weakness.
We do not know what we ought to pray for,
but the Spirit himself intercedes for us
with groans that words cannot express.

Romans 8:26

SEPTEMBER 2

Let us acknowledge the LORD;
    let us press on to acknowledge him.
As surely as the sun rises,
    he will appear;
he will come to us like the winter rains,
    like the spring rains that water the earth.

Hosea 6:3

MAY 1

"Forget the former things;
do not dwell on the past.
See, I am doing a new thing!
Now it springs up; do you not perceive it?
I am making a way in the desert
and streams in the wasteland," says the Lord.

Isaiah 43:18–19

SEPTEMBER 1

In the morning, O LORD, you hear my voice;
in the morning I lay my requests before you
and wait in expectation.

Psalm 5:3

MAY 2

We have put our hope in the living God, who is the Savior of all, . . . and especially of those who believe.

1 Timothy 4:10

AUGUST 31

No one has ever seen God;
but if we love one another,
God lives in us and his love
is made complete in us.

1 John 4:12

MAY 3

I will listen to what God the LORD will say;
he promises peace to his people, his saints.

Psalm 85:8

AUGUST 30

I lift up my eyes to the hills—
where does my help come from?
My help comes from the LORD,
the Maker of heaven and earth.

Psalm 121:1

MAY 4

May the God who gives endurance and encouragement give you a spirit of unity among yourselves as you follow Christ Jesus, so that with one heart and mouth you may glorify the God and Father of our Lord Jesus Christ.

Romans 15:5–6

AUGUST 29

The Lord holds victory in store for the upright,
he is a shield to those whose walk is blameless,
for he guards the course of the just
and protects the way of his faithful ones.

Proverbs 2:7–8

MAY 5

May the Lord direct your hearts into God's love and Christ's perseverance.

2 Thessalonians 3:5

AUGUST 28

May [you] have great endurance and patience, . . . joyfully giving thanks to the Father, who has qualified you to share in the inheritance of the saints in the kingdom of light.

Colossians 1:11–12

MAY 6

Trust in the LORD and do good;
dwell in the land and enjoy safe pasture.

Psalm 37:3

AUGUST 27

The LORD gives strength to his people;
the LORD blesses his people with peace.

Psalm 29:11

MAY 7

Cast your cares on the LORD
and he will sustain you;
he will never let the righteous fall.

Psalm 55:22

AUGUST 26

This is what the LORD says—
“Fear not, for I have redeemed you;
I have summoned you by name; you are mine.

Isaiah 43:1

MAY 8

He who fears the LORD has a secure fortress,
and for his children it will be a refuge.

Proverbs 14:26

AUGUST 25

If your heart is wise,
then my heart will be glad;
my inmost being will rejoice
when your lips speak what is right.

Proverbs 23:15–16

MAY 9

Jesus said, “Love each other as I have loved you. Greater love has no one than this, that he lay down his life for his friends.”

John 15:12–13

AUGUST 24

God has raised this Jesus to life,
and we are all witnesses of the fact.
Exalted to the right hand of God,
he has received from the Father
the promised Holy Spirit.

Acts 2:32–33

MAY 10

We were . . . buried with Christ through baptism into death in order that, just as Christ was raised from the dead through the glory of the Father, we too may live a new life.

Romans 6:4

AUGUST 23

May you be blessed by the LORD
the Maker of heaven and earth.

Psalm 115:15

MAY 11

Since we have been justified through faith, we have peace with God through our Lord Jesus Christ, through whom we have gained access by faith into this grace in which we now stand. And we rejoice in the hope of the glory of God.

Romans 5:1–2

AUGUST 22

I delight greatly in the LORD;
my soul rejoices in my God.
For he has clothed me with garments of salvation
and arrayed me in a robe of righteousness,
as a bridegroom adorns his head like a priest,
and as a bride adorns herself with her jewels.

Isaiah 61:10

MAY 12

The Lord makes me lie down in green pastures,
he leads me beside quiet waters,
he restores my soul.
He guides me in paths of righteousness
for his name's sake.

Psalm 23:2–3

AUGUST 21

I have fought the good fight, I have finished the race,
I have kept the faith. Now there is in store for me the crown
of righteousness, which the Lord, the righteous Judge,
will award to me on that day—and not only to me,
but also to all who have longed for his appearing.

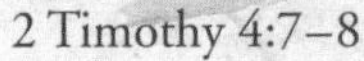

2 Timothy 4:7–8

MAY 13

Praise be to the God and Father
of our Lord Jesus Christ,
who has blessed us in the heavenly realms
with every spiritual blessing in Christ.

Ephesians 1:3

AUGUST 20

God who supplies seed to the sower
and bread for food will also supply
and increase your store of seed and will
enlarge the harvest of your righteousness.

2 Corinthians 9:10

MAY 14

Everything that was written
in the past was written to teach us,
so that through endurance
and the encouragement of the
Scriptures we might have hope.

Romans 15:4

AUGUST 19

Praise the LORD, O my soul,
and forget not all his benefits —
who forgives all your sins
and heals all your diseases.

Psalm 103:2–3

MAY 15

The LORD blesses the home
of the righteous.

Proverbs 3:33

AUGUST 18

Peacemakers who sow in peace
raise a harvest of righteousness.

James 3:18

MAY 16

The LORD himself goes before you
and will be with you; he will
never leave you nor forsake you.
Do not be afraid; do not be discouraged.

Deuteronomy 31:8

AUGUST 17

The Lord is my helper; I will not be afraid.
What can man do to me?

Hebrews 13:6

MAY 17

He who dwells in the shelter of the Most High
will rest in the shadow of the Almighty.
I will say of the LORD, "He is my refuge and my fortress,
my God, in whom I trust."

Psalm 91:1–2

AUGUST 16

The eyes of the LORD range
throughout the earth
to strengthen those whose hearts
are fully committed to him.

2 Chronicles 16:9

MAY 18

It is God who arms me with strength
and makes my way perfect.

2 Samuel 22:33

AUGUST 15

"Bring the whole tithe into the storehouse, that there may be food in my house. Test me in this," says the LORD Almighty, "and see if I will not throw open the floodgates of heaven and pour out so much blessing that you will not have room enough for it."

Malachi 3:10

MAY 19

My comfort in my suffering is this:
Your promise preserves my life, O Lord.

Psalm 119:50

AUGUST 14

A generous man will himself be blessed,
for he shares his food with the poor.

Proverbs 22:9

MAY 20

Cast all your anxiety on God
because he cares for you.

1 Peter 5:7

In Christ and through faith in him
we may approach God
with freedom and confidence.

Ephesians 3:12

MAY 21

Jesus said, "The knowledge of the secrets of the kingdom of heaven has been given to you. . . . Whoever has will be given more, and he will have an abundance."

Matthew 13:11–12

AUGUST 12

God will not let your foot slip—
he who watches over you will not slumber;
indeed, he who watches over Israel
will neither slumber nor sleep.

Psalm 121:3–4

MAY 22

God has rescued us from the dominion of darkness
and brought us into the kingdom of the Son he loves,
in whom we have redemption, the forgiveness of sins.

Colossians 1:13–14

AUGUST 11

God chose us in him before the creation of the world to be holy and blameless in his sight. In love he predestined us to be adopted as his sons through Jesus Christ, in accordance with his pleasure and will—to the praise of his glorious grace, which he has freely given us in the One he loves.

Ephesians 1:4–6

MAY 23

God's grace was given us in Christ Jesus
before the beginning of time.

2 Timothy 1:9

AUGUST 10

You . . . were included in Christ
when you heard the word of truth,
the gospel of your salvation.
Having believed, you were marked in him
with a seal, the promised Holy Spirit.

Ephesians 1:13

MAY 24

Flowers appear on the earth;
the season of singing has come,
the cooing of doves
is heard in our land.

Song of Songs 2:12

AUGUST 9

Do not be afraid.
Stand firm and you will see
the deliverance the LORD
will bring you today.

Exodus 14:13

MAY 25

Blessed are those who have learned to acclaim you,
who walk in the light of your presence, O LORD.

Psalm 89:15

AUGUST 8

Though I walk in the midst of trouble,
you preserve my life, O Lord.

Psalm 138:7

MAY 26

Blessed are all who fear the LORD,
who walk in his ways. . . .
Your sons will be like olive shoots
around your table.
Thus is the man blessed
who fears the LORD.

Psalm 128:1, 3–4

AUGUST 7

As long as the earth endures,
seedtime and harvest,
cold and heat,
summer and winter,
day and night
will never cease.

Genesis 8:22

MAY 27

The LORD is my shepherd, I shall not be in want.

Psalm 23:1

AUGUST 6

I will sing of your strength, O Lord,
    in the morning I will sing of your love;
for you are my fortress,
    my refuge in times of trouble.

Psalm 59:16

MAY 28

"Call to me and I will answer you
and tell you great and unsearchable things
you do not know," says the Lord.

Jeremiah 33:3

AUGUST 5

You are a chosen people, a royal priesthood,
a holy nation, a people belonging to God,
that you may declare the praises of him who called
you out of darkness into his wonderful light.

1 Peter 2:9

MAY 29

You know the grace of our Lord Jesus Christ,
that though he was rich, yet for your sakes
he became poor, so that you
through his poverty might become rich.

2 Corinthians 8:9

AUGUST 4

This is how God showed his love among us:
He sent his one and only Son into the world
that we might live through him.
This is love: not that we loved God,
but that he loved us and sent his Son
as an atoning sacrifice for our sins.

1 John 4:9–10

MAY 30

Posterity will serve the him;
future generations will be told about the Lord.

Psalm 22:30

AUGUST 3

In Christ we have redemption
through his blood, the forgiveness of sins,
in accordance with the riches of God's grace
that he lavished on us with
all wisdom and understanding.

Ephesians 1:7–8

MAY 31

Surely goodness and love will follow me
all the days of my life,
and I will dwell in the house of the LORD
forever.

Psalm 23:6

AUGUST 2

Those who have served well gain
an excellent standing and great assurance
in their faith in Christ Jesus.

1 Timothy 3:13

JUNE 1

The LORD loves the just
    and will not forsake his faithful ones.
They will be protected forever.

Psalm 37:28

AUGUST 1

The God of all grace, who called you
to his eternal glory in Christ,
after you have suffered a little while,
will himself restore you and make
you strong, firm and steadfast.

1 Peter 5:10

JUNE 2

Everyone born of God overcomes
the world. This is the victory
that has overcome the world, even our faith.

1 John 5:4

JULY 31

"If my people, who are called by my name,
will humble themselves and pray and seek my face
and turn from their wicked ways, then will I hear
from heaven and will forgive their sin
and will heal their land," says the Lord.

2 Chronicles 7:14

JUNE 3

My people will live in peaceful dwelling places,
    in secure homes,
    in undisturbed places of rest. . . .
How blessed you will be.

Isaiah 32:18, 20

JULY 30

O LORD, you have searched me
    and you know me.
You know when I sit and when I rise;
    you perceive my thoughts from afar.
You discern my going out and my lying down;
    you are familiar with all my ways.

Psalm 139:1–3

JUNE 4

This is the confidence we have in approaching God:
that if we ask anything according to his will, he hears us.
And if we know that he hears us—whatever we ask—
we know that we have what we asked of him.

1 John 5:14–15

JULY 29

It is God who makes . . . you stand firm in Christ.
He anointed us, set his seal of ownership on us,
and put his Spirit in our hearts as a deposit,
guaranteeing what is to come.

2 Corinthians 1:21–22

JUNE 5

Do not be anxious about anything, but in everything, by prayer and petition, with thanksgiving, present your requests to God. And the peace of God, which transcends all understanding, will guard your hearts and your minds in Christ Jesus.

Philippians 4:6–7

JULY 28

This is how we know what love is:
Jesus Christ laid down his life for us.

1 John 3:16

JUNE 6

Jesus said, "The Counselor, the Holy Spirit,
whom the Father will send in my name,
will teach you all things and will remind you
of everything I have said to you."

John 14:26

JULY 27

Perfume and incense bring joy to the heart,
and the pleasantness of one's friend
springs from his earnest counsel.

Proverbs 27:9

JUNE 7

A friend loves at all times.

Proverbs 17:17

JULY 26

The LORD is my strength and my shield;
my heart trusts in him, and I am helped.
My heart leaps for joy
and I will give thanks to him in song.

Psalm 28:7

JUNE 8

We . . . rejoice in God through
our Lord Jesus Christ,
through whom we have now
received reconciliation.

Romans 5:11

JULY 25

Because Jesus himself suffered
when he was tempted,
he is able to help those
who are being tempted.

Hebrews 2:18

JUNE 9

The LORD is good to those whose hope is in him,
to the one who seeks him.

Lamentations 3:25

JULY 24

In the beginning was the Word, and the Word was with God, and the Word was God. He was with God in the beginning. Through him all things were made; without him nothing was made that has been made. In him was life.

John 1:1–4

JUNE 10

How priceless is your unfailing love, O Lord!
Both high and low among men
find refuge in the shadow of your wings.

Psalm 36:7

JULY 23

No matter how many promises
God has made, they are “Yes” in Christ.
And so through him the “Amen”
is spoken by us to the glory of God.

2 Corinthians 1:20

Glory to God in the highest,
and on earth peace to men on whom his favor rests.

Luke 2:14

JULY 22

Christ was sacrificed once to take away the sins of many people;
and he will appear a second time, not to bear sin,
but to bring salvation to those who are waiting for him.

Hebrews 9:28

JUNE 12

Surely this is our God;
we trusted in him, and he saved us.
This is the LORD, we trusted in him;
let us rejoice and be glad in his salvation.

Isaiah 25:9

JULY 21

The LORD your God is with you,
he is mighty to save.
He will take great delight in you,
he will quiet you with his love,
he will rejoice over you with singing.

Zephaniah 3:17

JUNE 13

Jesus said, "Let the little children come to me,
and do not hinder them, for the kingdom of God
belongs to such as these." . . . And he took the children
in his arms, put his hands on them and blessed them.

Mark 10:14, 16

JULY 20

All your sons will be taught by the LORD,
and great will be your children's peace.

Isaiah 54:13

JUNE 14

Blessings crown the head of the righteous.

Proverbs 10:6

JULY 19

From the lips of children and infants
you have ordained praise, O Lord.

Psalm 8:2

JUNE 15

No eye has seen,
no ear has heard,
no mind has conceived
what God has prepared
for those who love him.

1 Corinthians 2:9

JULY 18

For God says,
"In the time of my favor I heard you,
and in the day of salvation I helped you."

I tell you, now is the time of God's favor,
now is the day of salvation.

2 Corinthians 6:2

JUNE 16

I praise you, Lord, because I am fearfully
and wonderfully made;
your works are wonderful,
I know that full well.

Psalm 139:14

JULY 17

From everlasting to everlasting
the LORD's love is with those who fear him,
and his righteousness with their children's children.

Psalm 103:17

JUNE 17

In my integrity you uphold me, Lord,
and set me in your presence forever.

Psalm 41:12

JULY 16

You will go out in joy
    and be led forth in peace;
the mountains and hills
    will burst into song before you,
and all the trees of the field
    will clap their hands.

Isaiah 55:12

JUNE 18

Jesus said, "I will see you again and you will rejoice, and no one will take away your joy."

John 16:22

JULY 15

Jesus said, "Where two or three come together in my name, there am I with them."

Matthew 18:20

JUNE 19

I waited patiently for the LORD;
he turned to me and heard my cry.
He lifted me out of the slimy pit,
out of the mud and mire;
he set my feet on a rock
and gave me a firm place to stand.

Psalm 40:1–2

JULY 14

By wisdom a house is built,
and through understanding it is established;
through knowledge its rooms are filled
with rare and beautiful treasures.

Proverbs 24:3–4

JUNE 20

The Lord gives strength to the weary
and increases the power of the weak.

Isaiah 40:29

JULY 13

Jesus prayed, "Holy Father,
protect [my followers] by the power
of your name—the name you
gave me—so that they
may be one as we are one."

John 17:11

JUNE 21

I pray that out of his glorious riches
God may strengthen you with power
through his Spirit in your inner being,
so that Christ may dwell
in your hearts through faith.

Ephesians 3:16–17

JULY 12

Jesus said, "My grace is sufficient for you,
for my power is made perfect in weakness."

2 Corinthians 12:9

JUNE 22

You will eat the fruit of your labor;
blessings and prosperity will be yours.

Psalm 128:2

JULY 11

The LORD is good,
  a refuge in times of trouble.
He cares for those who trust in him.

Nahum 1:7

JUNE 23

Jesus said, "By this all men
will know that you are my disciples,
if you love one another."

John 13:35

JULY 10

The righteous cry out, and the LORD hears them;
he delivers them from all their troubles.

Psalm 34:17

JUNE 24

The LORD is my light and my salvation—
whom shall I fear?
The LORD is the stronghold of my life—
of whom shall I be afraid?

Psalm 27:1

JULY 9

Your word is a lamp to my feet, O Lord,
and a light for my path.

Psalm 119:105

JUNE 25

Jesus said, "Do not let your hearts be troubled. Trust in God; trust also in me."

John 14:1

JULY 8

Jesus said, "So I say to you: Ask and it will be given to you; seek and you will find; knock and the door will be opened to you. For everyone who asks receives; he who seeks finds; and to him who knocks, the door will be opened."

Luke 11:9–10

JUNE 26

Let us not give up meeting together,
as some are in the habit of doing,
but let us encourage one another—and all
the more as you see the Day approaching.

Hebrews 10:25

JULY 7

God, who said, "Let light shine out of darkness,"
made his light shine in our hearts to give us the light of the
knowledge of the glory of God in the face of Christ.

2 Corinthians 4:6

JUNE 27

Jesus said, "To him who overcomes,
I will give the right to sit with me
on my throne, just as I overcame and
sat down with my Father on his throne."

Revelation 3:21

JULY 6

We have all had human fathers who disciplined us and we respected them for it. How much more should we submit to the Father of our spirits and live! Our fathers disciplined us for a little while as they thought best; but God disciplines us for our good, that we may share in his holiness.

Hebrews 12:9–10

JUNE 28

I know that the LORD saves his anointed;
he answers him from his holy heaven
with the saving power of his right hand.
Some trust in chariots and some in horses,
but we trust in the name of the LORD our God.

Psalm 20:6–7

JULY 5

God guides the humble in what is right
    and teaches them his way.
All the ways of the LORD are loving and faithful
    for those who keep the demands of his covenant.

Psalm 25:9–10

JUNE 29

The LORD confides in those who fear him;
he makes his covenant known to them.

Psalm 25:14

JULY 4

Blessed is the nation whose God is the LORD,
the people he chose for his inheritance.

Psalm 33:12

JUNE 30

A generous man will prosper;
he who refreshes others will himself be refreshed.

Proverbs 11:25

JULY 3

May the grace of the Lord Jesus Christ, and the love of God, and the fellowship of the Holy Spirit be with you.

2 Corinthians 13:14

JULY 1

Christ redeemed us from the curse of the law
by becoming a curse for us.

Galatians 3:13

JULY 2

If anyone acknowledges that Jesus is the Son of God,
God lives in him and he in God.

1 John 4:15